BRIEF
MORAL
HISTORY
IN BLUE

New Issues Poetry & Prose

Editor	Herbert Scott
Associate Editor	David Dodd Lee
Advisory Editors	Nancy Eimers, Mark Halliday, William Olsen, J. Allyn Rosser
Assistants to the Editor	Rebecca Beech, Marianne E. Swierenga
Assistant Editors	Erik Lesniewski, Carrie McGath, Lydia Melvin, Adela Najarro, Margaret von Steinen
Copy Editor	Dianna Allen
Editorial Assistants	Derek Pollard, Bethany Salgat
Business Manager	Michele McLaughlin
Fiscal Officer	Marilyn Rowe

New Issues Poetry & Prose
The College of Arts and Sciences
Western Michigan University
Kalamazoo, MI 49008

An Inland Seas Poetry Book

 Inland Seas poetry books are supported by a grant from The Michigan Council for Arts and Cultural Affairs.

First Edition, 2001

ISBN: 1-930974-07-8 (paperbound)

Library of Congress Cataloging-in-Publication Data:
Roberts, Beth
Brief Moral History in Blue/Beth Roberts
Library of Congress Catalog Card Number: 2001131165

Art Direction:	Tricia Hennessy
Design:	Sara Russell
Production:	Paul Sizer
	The Design Center, Department of Art
	College of Fine Arts
	Western Michigan University
Printing:	Courier Corporation

BRIEF
MORAL
HISTORY
IN **BLUE**

BETH ROBERTS

New Issues

WESTERN MICHIGAN UNIVERSITY

Contents

Acknowledgements

My thanks to the editors of journals which first published the following poems, some in earlier forms:

Another Chicago Magazine: "Year's End"

Black Warrior Review: "Horseshoe Crab"

Cimarron Review: "Worth"

The Gettysburg Review: "Blue Tick," "Cartoon," "Keep House"

Indiana Review: "Close"

The Iowa Review: "Mother"

New England Review: "The Narrow Escape"

Multitudinous gratitude also to the Illinois Arts Council, Cullen Bailey Burns, Joshua Clover, Lori Roderick, Lloyd Schoeneman, Drew Starenko and my extensive expansive family. Odd Nerdrum's paintings appear in *Round* and Tracy Emin's drawings in *Desire Right*. John Crowley is credited for the first sentence (and others like it) in *Near Miss*; Brenda Shaughnessy for doing a glossary; my niece Sophie for the last bit on pony, and finally, Rosalie and Ivan for the drive to care this much about the world.

Horseshoe Crab

The percussive God wears itself
out on a wall, where the moon
shows up blue in this king, pulling

us from our red show. Found on a beach,
scraping in the tide. Years, hundreds of
thousands it hummed to ocean

bottoms, settling the nadir
of its rising rings. Spit out on sand,
it blackened to an old tooth. But

to be one-limbed and round, perfectly
defunct intact within a circumference.
Surely the soul wouldn't bother to go,

but slowly shrink to the innermost
concentric circle of the body
the less alive it became,

spectacle vehicle, already in place.
To be priceless . . . a wheel, ring, pursed
lip or what is it the century requires.

Lives of Things

Disarray of the Still Life: you think you see light,
sifting through shadow, but if thought
could move an olive over, slightly, unsightly,
you might see more. So we are moved,

we eye our things. The beautiful ones look back.
They speak to us. Indeed, we will not leave
without our things. Alone in the house, radio off,
no relatives, we suspect them of both ambivalence

and evidence of us. Blemished minds:
who could guess a bracelet that fell from my wrist
would leave the human charm? What a dressed blue stain
would tell the watching world? What the clock told time?

In the Garden

Touching the blackberries in the dark
reminds me of some thing; to guess them
by the dimple, almost a thing not to touch,
a bee, little genitals of the pet, inevitably
the full-blown rose saturated in its own time,
disconcertingly heavy udder of color I can handle,
barely, touch itself the hinge, the thing
about flowers giving way, the imploring
shift to and away from the thought.

I know I will want to eat my children,
eat their bodies to reach them,
eat their ghosts to save them.
How not pluck and pluck
at the surefooted mien,
pure path of the voice, for
the gleaming thing in them,
the wise streak, the quick, like the dark
with a bright idea in a fantastic garden?

Nasturtium

All for the fingers: the part like money, the part for eating.
Lowdown and flattened to lawn for the profile, I figure

the leaves too round to nipple like poplar and less like change
than eucalyptus (sold cold to the winter nuptial). Opened,

the hot-colored flower—eye or mouth in turns—looks askant,
aware, ability on fire, a beauty so briefly delinquent.

Flexing blossom, acquiescent root, moving cursive in the dirt.
Edible scrawled there, from the sprawling mouth to the flower.

Tutti Frutti

Kids use candy to fill in spaces, gum together a day's incisors.
Touching the topic, we laugh—zotz, wacky wafers, tired

circus peanuts, fleshy pastel faux pas, but brief. Grown up,
we get more or less more. Strong or sad, both, addicted to the

hard candy of events, beyond the stretch with gaps of nothing next
to nothing to the day that rolls out a ticker-tape of sugar dots
        all in a row . . .

to the chocolate hour! of the day . . . what do we have of it? Enough
to laugh . . . laugh through a fault of one's one. Enough for now.

Keep House

Something's molting within this house all season,
monsoon or dry heat, every day I hop to repeat per
formance. I pick up the cast-off, make it stay

up, straighten the ruffed-up and tilted, the wilted
leaves, crooked horizon with eyes on the tv
I fix it all with open air and keep it there, still

the dust drapes and rots in socks, his ashes trail,
not tumbleweeds these with instruction per creation,
temperature and duration. The bottle

caps wanna be seeds. There's a hat rack in the hall
with something dead behind it. A bright spread
on the sofa that creeps off till I knife it

still over the gross abstraction beneath it.
Ugly bulk, calm yourself. What's here is clear.

There's a hole in the bucket, dear,

a river in the foyer. There's a heart in the kitchen
where you harried. There are souls in the closet
that are married, and twins in the coat

tree in the bedroom, albeit buried.

Cartoon

All the brittle sun slamming through the auto
mobile's invented and inflicted holes and rolled
down windows makes the eyes bug out like
a goofy joe, personoid staggering in a quick

passage—many ways to get lost in the cracks
between this reel and that reel, loud gaping laughter past
Good Humor Ice Cream's truck stopped dead on
I-80, in Iowa, on the third day past the Fourth.

What's more, there're many more caricatures shooting
by next door, some kind, others monstrous, all lost
in a twinkling of a river in a windowpane (air
conditioning). We comment on the make and model

while our hands grow huge. One grabs at bill
boards to halt the rocket's thought, minutely per
uses the new and next-to-new blueprints of probable
regrets, well, too easy to take off when you're still

at 80 mph, we might as well embrace the UFO,
the faster we'd go the more our lips would curl,
tears harden to horns with which to toss our kids
to a place where the arms could really soar.

Late Orpheus and Recent Eurydice

Now here is how we choose our way:
equal attention to purchasing—the car,
the christening dress, the wind-up
parking goddess—more than enough
supplied to what demands all this.

All this to get back. Daily we pay out
humility to surmise, respect to progress,
love to the far-flung. Fine-tuned we are
to balance, synchronizing steps, all
the right steps, *all together now* . . .

(We play our song, it keeps us going.)
You be Hi and I'll be Yo / you're behind
and I'm beyond / in between's
a bond . . .

Still (stunned by what's possible, besotted
with the daily fare, we suspect it is enough
for now, being kind) and blind,
gazing differently at profiles
on the coins we have for eyes.

The Orbit of Love

In the childhood memory of the prevision,
a field of yellow-centered flowers exhales
into a butter-colored house till everything
has an unctuous shine, reflecting its own
disappearance.

Next version: the vision spools out the house
window and rather than vistas sees voices,
licks up against something that sounds like big bucks.
Language, the spectrum of decision, led me here.

How far can one move into a house? To what extent
fall out of love, toward the memory of precision,
the yellowed memory. Surround-sound of worry,

while the carpenter finishes finishing the threshold
so the room itself can easily progress.

A Little Suspicion

Because I can imagine myself a life
under the burner, end in an oven
or trap, I'm not unsympathetic

to other energies running through
the house. Heedless of your least
thought, word or deed, I can

hold up your head, I can face your
face as you behold me, wondering
what tinkers in the kitchen,

what makes the mouse hairs
rise from the cutting board,
electricity in the face of gravity.

Thelma and Louise Saving Privates

begins with close focus on the big baby blues
of a certain protagonist uncertainly focusing
on her conflagratory past while blurring past
a burning semi semi-nude. She is tearing up
and tearing up the road, pow! emotion in motion,
but where's the boy? They will find him, she and
Louise, don't worry, if it's the last thing they do
together with their mini-gins and blitz crackers,
they'll get the boy and then spend Part 2 getting
rid of the boy since that's also what they do.
But if they could, they would keep him,
the three of them driving straight through a sunset,
Weather, Fun and Holy Past, a family finally.
But no, they don't get the boy, they never get it
enough with their two mouths always open
like that shrapnel will find them easier
than does comprehension of what it is he does,
losing body parts in that way that he does.

The Zone at the End of Summer

It takes three months just to wean yourself down
to the next lower level of nicotine. A forecast.

I drag the eyes across the long groan of the crops.
What do the Christian rockers do with a day like this?

The weather's severe clear but heaven's disappeared,
no, it's elsewhere, as the flood also is elsewhere

this evening. Past the violet elms, the dim herds,
it gnaws another place. Mississicky, chant the kids.

And while the radio duly cites its sick statistics
I wonder which is better, preferable rather: mud

in the eyes or to be the finest detail in a rite
of initiation. Does mud also fill the mouth

of an undiscovered grave? Is the rite a rape?
Turn here to make your decision.

Close

Devoting his life to child molestation,
he researches and writes. *Molestation,
child.* A station in life. He fell into it.
Maybe he was already shot—
nerves, blood—and impotent.
But those were his dreams that are orifices.
Those were openings, now gashes, worse,
gaps. All the rooms an office. Walls
the color of some girls.

He's learned some things from the other men
devoted to the issue (*sic*). Their hearts open
before they close in.
What great love doesn't arrive
with a shade of malcontent,
doesn't arrive. They love the small skin.
The palpable hearts, so close, like words.
The unearthly display when
time, it seems, disagrees.

But time stops only to switch beliefs.
Take a beach, he says, a day rife
with light and children laughing.
The grand possibility of it all, all
the futures winking like waves.
Take the sudden impossibility, the chill
at the thought. Take the wordless thought,
the love it takes to move the thinker.
This process, he says, it works.

The Narrow Escape

During the station break, a memory
straddles a few lengths of space-time
and jeers. I try the picture:

an extreme blonde five (splayed hand), I covered
the eight blocks from school-home in self
preservation, the route a hydrant, the living

room a glued-up bone china reindeer.
Focus in: once a wide car sidled
up close, leaned over and said it knew

my folks and I'd have a ride home.
There was the candy involved. I watched
the smile and wondered what kind.

As the smile opened slow and wide, inward
flew a raggy bird and its piece of sky, a million
trillium, cough against the forest floor, spinning

leaf, a rodeo, television mirrored
in a picture window, an expanse of ice,
a voice. I guess it was no, since

I walked faster in time to no, no, no, no
and overcame the hydrant as he pulled
away, sighing. I should have liked to

review him as plucked off by the rush,
but it was a small town.
Very small on its hill in the sky blue sky.

Mother

I was thinking you'd call when the flood came
though I know it was worse in Ohio still
this state empties out into vowels too
like bayou and poor one and lucky

Drew's gone out to get some stuff it's late
I was late coming home with the truck
again he said he knew it would happen
I was going to sell encyclopedias to a farmer

over in Cordova for a few bucks for once
I watched the sun wander and tripped you
could smell it all over the fields where the furrows
secreted and I passed one deer crossing

sign and thought of you it's true I did
forget the time in all that wrinkled air
and rabbits buzzing in the ditches I could've
gone all evening and never found the farmer

Your Keep

Only one who knows the body with skill and invention,
counsel, wheedle, blood, loosening arms, might
be more aware of the harm to do children.

Before you were the usual misgivings, missing parts born
or the whole child done, daily informant on the radio
to make a season's best gone bad,

but look . . . now you're here with a mouthful and a look, easy
to make happy, or already happy and so to make last.
I put your foot to my lips and make you laugh, place

a hand across your chest, I try to keep you in this place.
There is a mind in the gap at the small of my back: no art
and no artillery, no heart will keep you so

Burned House

The bad neighbors in the insulation-colored house who shot
the sky, drank brunch and burned whatever was at hand
have burned the hand that held them.

Dog sniffs new snow at the perimeter while I
admire the debris under the moon. Under the weather
the structure looks askant, less blatantly black & blue

at night. Off the porch, a chair holds ash that held
the arsonist with a new vision of home.
I put my nose to the house for the view:

on the coldest day in eighty years, a slim shoot appeared
in a dull light. Disenchanted with all his bright ideas,
he got the family out. Details condensed to a blue tip

on a minute finger, enlightened.
Then it was only a matter of time and matter.
Domestic fire licked everything shaped.

I lay the varied planes of my face against the wood
to feel it still. A faint smell, as in singed paper, as in
far controlled burns at the end of the day.

Something to Burn

Wake up, all the senses rapacious, like one
who's been had. Cigarette rolls over
on its side, stunted as the actor to its double,

fat man in a fat space, nothing to hide.
But someone has something in mind to hide.
Stars squeeze up to a special relativity,

sure mc², cig with a swirl, I was a girl
looking for sex in the starry night and went
for a song, waltzed up to a jukebox with a couple

coins and quit with the news and a mess of
hard cash. I'd like to sell an anger I harbor.
It could get you somewhere good, like—

an arbor. And that fresh house in the clear
ing clear of meaning begs the question:
is it love in the view of the arsonist?

What's left but to waive it like a cynic,
entirely modern survivor, or rage, rage
at the unwavering image. Unless it does

waver, does change, begs a creator, first light,
then heat, then the whole shiny baby of it
burning clear as a song concerning you.

Blue Tick

Having opened to your face closed up in sun
glasses once, I raze the news daily for more of you.

These days it's pornography mainly, moth vs.
the light, the question being who lied

and who lies still. I've learned from headlines giving
head and the heads of state we'd better be either

bug or divine to survive with a semblance of being seen.
I must have failed you, hence the glasses and fabric

ated name of a girl running along
the edge. I would think such a thing, lying

as it occurs, I make my day a cursed
Sunday, no church, no meal, I get you

from the news, the same sky mud-slinging
among us, gibbous, dog stars, all laughing

at us at once and the same place. Hence you're
on the east or west coast, and nowhere

between, face blue from the twitching
screen, thinking mostly—I see it

like a sunspot—of a world emptied out of a box
by sex, debriefed population all alone with their parts

and wondering. And now the moon,
with whom we share a responsibility.

And now the silence, the ticks in the walls and tick-
tock toward the light. So you see how I long

for you, prurient in the ribs of the hired hound,
slight sycophant fattening on absence.

Crash Course

Something to do with time and space, slip in the warp, halt in
  the tick,
but it feels like more than lack, doesn't it, feels like taking time
  straight.

I've seen lightning illuminate night's convexo-concave all night,
heavy with summer heat and with edges burning take the sky
  beyond

its perimeter, while along the highway's slow declination the
  arrow of the car
fell far. But in the world there are hard and fast rules concerning
  boundaries.

So far I've had bad pain, needed drink, and made myself hungry
  for looks.
And it may be vanity, finally, that claims the vehicle. But where
  was my head

that afternoon, with children at every window? And the time
  before that?
Time before that? . . . so heavy in thought that the body blew off

or weightless with thought while the body stayed, the blind
  body, traffic
on traffic, seducing a balance that held its sway with a mind on
  you till traffic

snapped and got away. Again the baby cries, a little unhurt,
  unwilling arena
for memory. Again some mechanism turns over

Mise en Scène

I see Jeanne, mise en scène, *k-i-s-s, in her head* . . .
or is it *on her head*, the part where the cross,
the crossing begins? I've spent the better part

of an afternoon crossing a ditch, the same
ditch to and fro, putting myself in place.
If I had a horse I would keep going, accomplice

to his mission. Simple friction, the animal of guilt
with animal of grace, ganging on the horizon.
And the ground between would be her armor—

I mean honor—armor. Those licked by God,
what do they wear? When Joan put on fire,
did she weather the world inside her?

Truth is my car sped past the ditch while I
pictured the rest. I caught the weed snap
and was there, wet at the heels, butting the air.

Not chosen. Nor choosing to bend back, back
bent, nonetheless.

Mind Makeup

The mind's not distinct till you make it so,
made up of everything under the sun,
the sun, other bodies heavenly, illovely . . .

bore a hole in the mind, staring at the sun,
scrutinizing any other object, one
of any number of objects in a field, or the field . . .

the attraction a clearcut border
around which to arrange your arrangements,
the concomitant trickles of your enterprise.

But if what you have in mind is ill-conceived?
Too late then for the love tap, innocence,
too late for the hallelujah and halloo. . . .

But if you change your mind? . . . poor thing,
the shape of the mind's the same shape
as the quell of the sun's prefigured blow.

Year's End

Avoiding relation I go for the throat.
In the sifting traffic hourglass heart

things appear thinned, limbs in the dance
separate in the new circumstance.

Where the edge of a hand slips to the field
is a synapse so fine, yet all the world

wants a long attenuating history in its stead.
Snowflakes pivot through the gap. In my head

I repeat till it beats, I love all my loves, I love
all my love,

Near Miss

In winter summer's a myth. Amiss.
I had breasts and beneath them, ribs
long as Abel's wonder, now this.

See the jagged horizon across
the cleaned chest? There a creature lives
in winter. Summer's a myth. A Miss

something or other nurse who bets
on the horses and has a debt list
long as Abel's wonder . . . now this

morning she says, *Look at this*:
You are full of your own moments.
In winter summer's a lisp, shhhh,

I see the heart, my genie genesis,
doling out its furled concentrics
long as Abel's wonder. Now this

was like a kiss, a series.
Him beating me to the grass.
In winter summer's a myth amiss,
a long and able wonder. Now this.

The Real Thing

When the winter sun wakes a snake it jumps the gun.
Unhinged by a preternatural spring, the kids

and I tried the snowshot hill right before our eyes.
In the snow three ovoid boys made a man, boy being

father to the man, while we wrote in the snow
Rosalie, mom, uncanny and fresh with overuse

as the real red rose. What I thought too soon
was too late, fireworks that made a sunlick strike

were fake and the real thing made a man cool
into slush beneath a car, me to spin the kids into a tree.

The one deciduous in all the field, the biggest of the boys
flattened and flung *get down you idiots you're gonna get shot*

to the two maybe smaller for still downhill
and caught in the waves of sound, not shot down.

January

Here is the body of the year,
lying like the land does.

If we raging in the beginning
wanna big band with a bold bang

no one should be blamed.
Afterward, imbricate

snow scores the road,
space and thin words.

I cross a rural landscape this
year as I did last, and see

very little, curling round
the root of tenderness.

Tangential North

The most lascivious landscape I've seen—
a freezing highway of storm-dissembled vehicles
lapping the space
between freeway and field.

If I put my finger on it, in part it's violent.
Northern pike sweeping up to the duck.
Sunset, firearms, calls struck
out across the water, winter.

Across seven moving bodies of water
the only thing still is a hummingbird.

Still on the tile, a partridge breast plucked,
another nude of the heart,
traffic pulse, muscle to flex . . . *buzz asleep,*
sleep abuzz . . . deep in the automaton chill.

Round

Was that a little music, there
in the kinked cloud, hooked
in the fold?

There in the hanging tree,
in the white bent knee
pinking up the dawn,

horizon strung, high
tenor weather, plucked affair.
Was that a little music, there

Raised Up

From the dual fists of the church, small and white,
you understand the stuff of beauty

dripping Jesus to be (in the flesh *understand*, hand-
to-mouth *understanding*) as a page, dissolving undeserved.

And as you empty the thought or fill the feel,
you surround the hole of the mouth that wells up

and understand: Jesus in the middle of the night,
star-crossed on a high road with a mouthful of this.

Desire Right

One artist at the show (T. Emin) got desire right:
pen stroke slash & blur make a burrow from the brain:
1.) action couched in thought, 2.) trajectory, 3.) wake.

Course, she's really a storyteller and brings her pen
to pain, as in *Everything I want belongs to you*,
trailing a small scrawl of the sad thing she does own.

(If I trace his body with both hands in a dream,
this is not the same as the outline of desire . . .
to open your heart, you make it incomplete . . . right?)

My own girl draws wind lashes with a silver glitter pen.
They flap and flare open, silver lining in the outskirts
of desire! They do look like the wind

The Cutting Edge

Whether you say Look, two dead squirrels
or Lovers who fell from a tree,
what does it matter, driving the kid to school?

One you got death, two you got sex and death,
both a lotta onomatopoeia to buttress morning
kindergarten. And where in this case, class,

is the difference in I love you or I love my serrated life?
One you got platitude, two you got pathos, both
plenty of not much. Say I, um, hum him, or somesuch.

Moon over the Time 'n Space Drive-In

It all began at the Time 'n Space Drive-In.
So one weekend at the end of the season
we drove over between day and night,
this time not looking for a good time,
but to see the full moon stare while we
watched them do it or who dunnit, lit

from nearer afield. Space was filling.
Still, we made it up the middle.
What lacked organic forged mechanic.
There for the moon, I secretly hoped
for a Western. We tuned to the cartoon,
The Lemonheads, and bought the candy hearts.

The film was noir but the moon a romance.
I fell into a light sleep, the stuff of light years,
till the heart in my mouth snapped
in two: *Who do / voodoo?*
I looked at you. Man-in-the-moon blue.
Shot hero, still shooting Stars.

Learning to Spell

All the difference between Illinois
and Island hangs before us

like the task of trying to place
a pendulum. Still, while I pace

entire pastures of palindrome,
ever clever clover, still

you (girl with a likeness to space
around the I) spell

Give it Up

In spring the sudden snarl of profusion
coerces me into blaming the neighbors.
There are too many of us. In the union
of winter we kept to our labor,

small room to err in the house of the body
locked in a warehouse of weather.
In the one spare room, precious fodder
gets to the heart of the matter.

But when the needles prick the surface,
fulvous larvae, hooded rhododendron
heart-shaped leaves us loving commerce.
Goddish sprouts attempt the garden.

I would like to meet them all,
the children filling up the park.
If only I could know you well,
half-filled killer beyond the bark,

before you begin to turn me in.
If I yield to higher standards,
the field will open
to the naked eyes' double standards,

barely a gloss over the fault.
Look at the yard, it's an open wound
that heals all day, and under the vault
of heaven gives up its longing, lost in found.

Worth

On a day fresh as a haircut
I left the family for the field.
I looked hard for the body.

Where drifts of light leaned
into pockets of rot, of not, in fact,
it was best. There were words

in the woods: shiver   for needles,
veinous   for moss, matter
for the hour or the forest floor.

Whether they were well spent
depends on their worth. But
while ether disentangled

the antlers and the roots, there
was one note. With a hint
of meaning, being bent.

In the voice of a bird. One
clean run through to the night,
and it sounded like   new.

It sounded like   you.
I found the body, looking,
and it cost too much.

Could You Find it in Your Heart

Pacing the treeline during the interim,
listening to shifts in the snow, clicking
water, weather hides well, the state
of precipitation and its lack is invisible,
though it asks for the long gaze.
No better rest for the eye than the weather,
like no better place for the heart than

the body: what water, what matter,
insidious traps, commerce and failure.
Let out, the heart enlarged leaps to detail,
pries overcast for the red sprig, wig, vein,
smile. It's always there, though we can't
believe it, the hand on the heart, the heart
in the throat.

A Thing of Beauty

Where did we put that beautiful thing,
now we need it? All of a sudden,
sodden with time and hosting some
emissary of disease or worse,
yes now, we're desirous of that thing,
surely it wasn't the imagination.

Let's look through the house of memory,
but look, already it's built of cards.
We'll look at the cards, then, the moon,
the fool, the hanging man! Let's go outside,
something was out here under the sun,
a thing of beauty, growing from your hand,

or purchased through your spending, or made,
or found, outside the machination. It's possible
there is no word for it. You sit and wait, then.
I'll go find a field, and fold the field in two.
All the beautiful things therein I'll pour
into the smaller fold of you.

Concentration

The weight on that mountain masters its own,
what remains under what remains. We enter

by the road sign of the dense, but fairy-figured,
carved convicted pointing *to the Quarry.*

(Of the other, *to Buchenwald* with a grinning
collared bear, only a photo remains.)

At the gate a flicker of stink, taken
by distance: rivers of hills, towers of spires.

And the foreground's stuffed with a wreck
array, rectangular imprints of barracks.

At the end of the war all citizens of Weimar
were marched up the mountain and made

to look: what they saw in the way
of their shivers of hills, liars of spires,

what rained, seeped into their footfalls.
And who remained saw the looks of them.

Five o'clock, the luxurious hour said *go,*
but I was locked on a thimble in a glass case,

lost or left, now annotated. I looked into it:
recurring iris, vivisection, every spring

a new laboratory, new spell, what recurs, remains . . .
Fascination cupped this thing, this gleam,

for a hint of sense in its gape,
what wind was left just under its lip . . .

and got the wall of smell from the gate.
All the heft in a fingertip.

First Map

I lived once in a long landscape, with much in it.
Stones trembled in the mounting water, rivers
of fleshstone splayed across the glacial valley, lakes
brightened their reflection, fish rose above their lives,

cliffwalls pulsed across stages of weather, falling
to the rolling sound, winding into forests of molded,
gilded floors and glittering ceilings, and the sidelong depths.
I was enlarged by the place, thus more myself in it.

Later a prelude brought it back, waterfall
of increments. I thought to make a map:
Step . . . to locate the landscape. Stop . . . to feed
from the beating distance. Swim . . .

God's Country

From four lanes to two, two by two in four by fours,
We come to the calendar place, October, the screen
Saver behind our eyes, poplars ticking, the dream.
Lucky to be born in God's Country, I return on all fours,
All the better to kneel. All the better to see what's reflecting
In the eye of one of a thousand bodies of water. It's mud,
This close. Could be clay. Ashes, dust. Where's God?
Applause from trees, yea, intermittent praise all genuflecting
Evening. I crawl down a road, I listen to the wind, I listen
To the frogs, I listen to a distant accident, the road home
Attenuates to darkness with a faint *plink* at the horizon.
When a birch begins to glow, I eve-dream it limbs, some
One good as God in *God vs. Nature*, where He says, "Some
One's coming . . . a pilgrim, bright of body, nor dumb."

Instrumental

Dwelling in the body there's too much thoughtless air.
Down a path to a clear headstone lives the life of the mind.

Love's the birthmark on the brain, a song-shaped stain.
Or, orchestrated shocks that make the heart beat back.

Eli,

for Eli William Roderick
lived 9/15/93

first you were born, then
lived a time, a very short time, a life
with the look of a mayfly left
a petrified forest in me.

You must be excused,
(you didn't have everything
you needed) and God.
(First I was everything you needed.)

(As though) first again I was left
in full form a winged lack, black
velocity, wind without
hitch to black out or elide

or fix what dropped you,
the very air. Only now I see
you've made of me a bird
among leaves, hundreds

of feathers like minute fingernails
but no real wings nor need
for wings with my kind . . .
and the small of my back,

former way of harms,
you've displaced with another,
fully formed of heft,
sweet, bit, resident.

Scene, Not Heard

Joseph's eyes are so light blue you doubt they see
well, they swirl and mote, brief flexing ghosts.
They sway around the best built truths like the best metaphors,
the worst. When he sees a red rose

against a wall, there is the wall where none rise.
Red rose in all the eyes imprisoned and otherwise
in Yugoslavia and other former places during his war.
Wary and late for another frontier, he drinks German coffee

and worries about our scattered boys, no strength
on the front. Don't apprise him of the new biological
front, don't make it real, he's been listening to you
for 88 ears, and he's heard enough, too.

True to Form

Every eve the tilt back of the head to cloud
sunsettling thought, shh, aim to be true.
The cap of one's personal evening.

What do you put on and what retract
to get that blue: *mistress distress*, the newest
shade, something will be made of that, a sky . . .

What would you do to disguise your hunch,
what discover. What process of illumination
to undress, which piety, whose starry eye . . .

Brief Moral History in Blue

We began the march with our best brights and bust rights,
safe in the surety of the good bluebook of acclaim, wherein

the sky is a hint of the same everlasting, fluctuating
imprint of a blue fuck and its long impression of night.

Consciousness, town crier in a sleepy sleeping city of tendril
and mongrel and scoundrel, is dreaming of the body

awake and bell-eyed to the least bruise of heaven, when
really awake to lie down in shadow, undo the brief skein.

Asked if I'd do it again, grim darling, I'd say the same thing
(in a shade deeper blue understanding all over) again.

Loss Glossary (Abbrev.)

AFTERBIRTH

Second born, of premature heft and a hundred red,
in the air and on the bed, maps where God slid.

LEGS

Air where they were
flexing doubled, God-red.

KEYS

Extensions of the digits,
especially index,
pinkie clink.

MIND

A day so white, what did it matter
I wanted a little red.

WAR

Too red meant we were losing and losing it.

MEMORY

Lost too, we were meaning and meant it.

BABY

I knew you when you were alone
in your father's mind, and,
milli-faceted gem, demolition,
a child's desk, red.

OBJECT

Saddled and bridled Asian horse, two inches
high, jade and gold, nostrils flared red.

MELODY
Fabricate with a bright thread running through it.

LIST
A small thing to save me, written in my body, and read there.

Perfect Machine

The makers of the perfect machine understood
memory: in the beginning were the good
voices that bevelled our eyes and filled
our ears at ground level with the world's
own curvature,
gave us the lure
of touch; and at the other end grief,
the need—gang bang at Lethe—
to be the death of grief.

The perfect-machine-makers had read
up on remembrances: from our parents' bed
to the risk we take when we mistake
night for a meadow, a gale for a lark.
What imagination!
In commemoration
of faulted hearts they tilted the machination
of love—imperfect provision—
toward a more perfect improvisation.

Those who made the machine perfect knew,
concerning souvenirs, a thing or two.
We want the parts of the body to wear,
like those gilded strands of Shire's hair
stolen from the field
where the horses yield
all day their quivering hides to the lonely.
They drew our field of vision out from
the field. Go and find your own piece of pony.

photo by Jay Strickland

Beth Roberts was born in Chicago in 1965 and grew up in Michigan's Upper Peninsula. After graduate work at the Iowa Writers' Workshop, she moved to Rock Island, Illinois, where she lives with her husband and children.

New Issues Poetry & Prose

Editor, Herbert Scott